To, Karen

With my love,

Annie x

Listen to my Heart

An Anthology of Life, Love and Loss

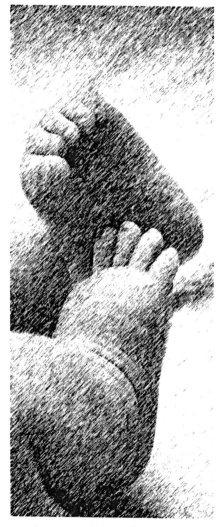

Annie Watkinson

AuthorHouse™ UK Ltd.
500 Avebury Boulevard
Central Milton Keynes, MK9 2BE
www.authorhouse.co.uk
Phone: 08001974150

First published by AuthorHouse 2/21/2008

ISBN: 978-1-4343-5781-6 (sc)

Printed in the United States of America
Bloomington, Indiana

This book is printed on acid-free paper.

authorHOUSE®

Dedication

This book is dedicated
to
my remarkable family,
Mike, Joanna, Ian and Rebecca.

And to
Amelie, William and Daniel,
my reason to live;
and keep on living.

Contents

Introduction ix

Listen to the World's Pain

To the People of Dunblane 3

Hell on Earth? 5

Renewal 7

The Midwife 9

H.I.V. 10

Hepatitis C 11

Listen to the Mind's Pain

The Wounded Healer 15

The Case Conference 16

Dementia 18

Life Goes On 20

Inside the Madness 21

I'm Me 22

The Stalker 24

Get Up and Go! 27

For You 29

Healing? 31

The Secret Life 33

The Lonely Heart 34

The Exposed Heart 36

Please? 37

She Sits Alone... 39
To a World in Which Failure is Unacceptable ... 41
Act 1 Scene 1 42

Listen to the Love of a Family

For My Mother R.I.P. 45
Monsters in the Garden.................................. 46
Did I Remember to Tell you? 48
Daniel... 50
William... 51
For Sweet Amelie 52
Hush Little Child 53
My Child, The Man 55

Listen to the Pain of Cancer

Together 59
New Life for Old 61
A Cancer Captive 62
A New Season's Hope 64
Sorry 65

Listen to My Faith

On Giving and Receiving 69
The Only True Way.. 71
Hope is a Flower 73
The Sower... 74
Rest Awhile 76

Introduction

❧ ❧ ❧

Poetry is not something that I have to work at. Poems have the audacity to insist on being written. They invade my sleep, my waking hours, my moments of leisure and work. They give me no peace until the ink has been spilt onto paper.

These poems are experiences of life; both my own and of others I have had the privilege of coming alongside through my nursing and also through my pastoral work in a church setting.

I have battled with my own physical and mental distress, and I am currently fighting breast cancer.

Many of the people I have cared for have struggled with depression, dementia and delusions. Others have been the victims of physical, sexual and mental abuse, and find it hard to ever trust again. Many have struggled with addiction; to substances, behaviours and even to people. Still more have had to suffer unbearable physical pain and chronic illness.

Poetry is subjective, which is why a verse can touch the heart and soul far more easily than a thousand word essay. What I hope for you, the reader, is that you may identify with, and be comforted by the rhythm and rhyme of the verses contained in this book. Some poems may seem bleak, others hopeful, but there is reality contained within each line, and they may reassure you that you are never alone in suffering. Others have been there before, even though your own experience of suffering is as individual as a fingerprint. We are all part of a big organisation called 'Life'.

Listen to the World's Pain

No man is an island.
We all share in his pain.

To the People of Dunblane

On 13th March 1996 16 children and their teacher, Gwen Mayer, were killed in 3 minutes of carnage. The attacker then committed suicide.

I wish you comfort,
But I know
My hopeless dream cannot contain
Your overwhelming pain,
And you would wish no need for comfort.

I wish you peace,
God knows, Yet foolish words.
No peace in loss,
In struggling to cope with devastation;
In fear that bitterness will overwhelm, engulf you.

I wish you hope,
A senseless metaphor.
God knows the bleakness of your thoughts;
A community robbed of priceless angels.
Hopelessness tears at the very fabric
That holds your mind together,
Till in fragments you wish your soul could explode.

I wish you God.
God knows.
God cares.
Who knows?
We care.
Repair will happen;
Not perfect joins,
But ragged edges,
A patch placed on an exudating wound.
And soon
A smile
Maybe,
From the face of an angel
Here on earth.
Rebirth of love.
Not yet awhile,
But soon.
Till then we all continue to pray
For you, our friends.

Hell on Earth?

I watched TV last night.
Maybe I shouldn't;
This world is full
Of drunken violence, rapes, abductions, hate.
Of children abandoned
On streets of dust.
Mothers too weary, too worn out
With poverty and sadness,
Droughts, floods, storms.
Of decent people
Stabbed in their back yards,
And men and women
Shocked, too shocked to care
For one more murder,
One more case of lust.
Mistrust building up in
Communities, fearful
Of their neighbours.

War torn streets and broken promises;
Of soldiers, young, confused,
Too young to die,
And lost,
Not knowing whose battle
They are fighting,
Bombs exploding.

Surely Armageddon could not be worse?

Renewal

❧ ❧ ❧

Safe beneath the bandage
The wound begins to heal,
Fibroblasts migrating
'Cross the vast and bloody weal.
Granulating tissues
Restoring damaged skin,
Exudate and pus build up,
Bacteria moves in,
Proteus, klebsiella,
Staphylococcus aureus;
Lymphocytes and monocytes
Fight battle glorious.
Platelets and factor
Build artistic scaffolding,
Whilst in the depths
Red blood cells surge,
Renewal to begin.

And under the soft covers,
'Neath such tender loving care,
Was the scar
Now forming nicely,
Made of exudate and air.
And if only,
In this world today
Renewal could begin,
'Neath the canopy
of God's cast sky,
To rid the world of sin.

The Midwife

When working in a maternity unit, I was distressed when dealing with two mothers in opposite rooms of the corridor. One mother had to give birth to a much-wanted baby knowing he was already dead. The other mother already had two healthy little boys and desperately wanted a girl. When the baby was born, perfectly formed and healthy, his mother turned on her side and rejected him.

I saw a baby born today,
I saw another die,
'Twas just a tiny stillborn child,
I watched the mother cry.
I watched, and cried along with her,
Such wretched tears of grief,
The fruits of labour ripped away,
As death came, like a thief.

I saw a baby born today,
It was a baby boy,
His mother prayed to have a girl,
So this child gave no joy.

H.I.V.

In 1995, I spent several months working as a volunteer at a children's A.I.D.'s hospice. The children were wonderfully cared for, but several died in such a short time. Thankfully this has changed now with the advent of new antiretroviral drugs, which increase life expectancy considerably.

Don't you want to play with me?
Dance with me, and sing?
Even though I'm H.I.V.,
And I'll be dead by spring.

Hepatitis C

Five thousand people in the UK were infected with the hepatitis C virus through contaminated NHS blood products, given as part of their treatment. Lord Robert Winston described it as "the worst treatment disaster in the history of the NHS." Many people were not told that they had been infected until years later.

Contamination seeped,
Slipped under skin like velvet,
Penetrating soft folds of silk.
Surreptitious,
Under the pretence of correction;
Partaking opportunities
Not afforded to other less fortunate viruses.
Upon invitation to a host.

Innocence corrupted,
Mother injected,
Father fostered hope.

Time marches on.
The invasion continues to multiply,
Basking in hidden cells,
As leech-like
It gains its advantage,
From non-understanding,
So undemanding,
It makes its own way;
Mother dejected,
Father lost hope.

Listen to the Mind's Pain

Listen not for the screaming, but for the silence of the tormented soul.

The Wounded Healer

The empathy comes naturally,
She knows their pain too well.
For she has suffered too, you see.
The scars are there,
Visible,
If you take the time to observe;
The ragged wounds,
The tattered soul,
The million unshed tears.
Catch the smell of terror,
The bitter taste of fear.
Can't you see
She carries her own pain,
While bearing the load of others?
And as you watch her walk towards
A dying, hurting world,
She will stand alongside fearlessly,
Tend to them compassionately,
Bathe their wounds so carefully;
Provide pillows for their aching head,
An outlet for their grief,
Soft words for their anxieties,
And wrap them underneath
The blanket of her tender loving care,
Because she has been there.

The Case Conference

The case conference begins,
And I rock in my chair,
Doctors, nurses and carers,
So many people are there!
They discuss my behaviour, appearance,
My fears,
They fire questions at me,
I break down in tears.
They take this as evidence
Of unsound mind,
So I just leave the room,
Leave my freedom behind.
Intimidation complete,
I give in to my grief,

The section's upheld,
I'm unable to leave.
Can't they all see
That I'm sad, not insane?
But it will be three more months
For another chance to gain
My freedom.

I may be dead by then,
Will they care?
As another inmate
Takes their turn
In the chair.

Dementia

❦ ❦ ❦

I see you shuffling clumsily
Along the hospital corridor,
And when I look into your eyes
I see a vacuum.
You look,
But you don't recognise me.
Just a hollow empty stare.
Yet you were once
An eminent surgeon,
Loyal friend,
Loving husband and father,
Until dementia.
The nurses who care for you,
They look so young!
They call you 'darling'
As they take your arm.

I speak sharply;
'He is Dr Jones, please.'
Eminent surgeon,
Loyal friend,
Loving husband and father,
Until dementia.
Incontinent, mumbling, shuffling, stumbling,
You have no idea
Of who you are,
Or who we are.
My poor mother lost her husband
Years ago,
And now we must await that second death,
When we can finally mourn,
As your body joins your soul
Already departed,
And this shell of a man crumbles.
Yet it once contained
That eminent surgeon,
Loyal friend,
Loving husband and father,
Until dementia.
A cruel, dual death.

Life Goes On

I tried to rid myself last night, of life,
But you can see
It would not go away.
The yellow pills piled high
And ochre bright, just ten; a dozen more,
Washed down with golden wine,
To gently ease the path
From this life's strain.

I felt the lightness form inside my head,
I swayed beneath soft lights
Of amber pale.
Closed eyes, heavy from the tranquilizer's pressure, as
Red veins appeared,
A tangled motorway
Of a frayed existence.
Morning came, a soft dawn, gently lit
With summer sun, pure yellow,
In sky of azure blue.
No mortuary grey,
Or blackened coffin mine,
For the time being anyway.
'Life goes on' or so they say,
Till next time,
Come what may.

Inside the Madness

Like an express train
At full speed,
My mind accelerates,
Corners taken recklessly;
Carriages full with busy commuters
Each with their own agenda,
Until, speeding round bends
The train derails, and dreams,
Like carriages spill.
Fresh blood upon torn and twisted metal.
Screaming and sobbing,
Echoes from within
Trapped memories, ruined hopes,
Mutilated ambitions.
Sirens approaching from a distance
With hypodermics
Ready,
But the sick cannot be treated,
Just patched up and sent to trudge their way along
Another set of dusty, rusty rails.
Feet blistered,
Heart broken,
Head in turmoil,
Life ruined
By the vehicle of madness.

I'm Me

What are you asking for,
That I cannot give?
That I cannot live
A life to its full.

What are you grasping for?
An answer unknown,
So I stumble alone
As life takes its toll.

What are you demanding?
I have nothing left,
I feel so bereft,
It's not possible.

What are you looking for?
I cannot measure
Up to this image you treasure;
A human idol.

Why won't you let me be
The person I am?
But this battering- ram
Demands so much more.

I'm just me, imperfect,
Hopeless, impossibly useless.
Just me,
You see?

The Stalker

The phone rings,
Echoes in the early morning air.
Just one, no more.
Emotions tense,
As time makes sense
Of the stalkers mark.
No number recall,
How unusual!

But chaos starts
Within the heart
And hands of the receiver.
Confusion reigns OK.
Success for the man on the end
Of the line,
As damped down cinders of fear
Flare into a dangerous flame.
To respond or to ignore?
Or wait,

Another morning, another call,
Confirming instincts,
As clock hands creep
To the appointed time, upon the wall.

A fleeting glimpse,
No more.
Nerve ends strain, alert and raw.
She dances to his tune,
Success is gained.
For years she's been trained
For this.
Defences now come crumbling down.
She hesitates,
But now responds.
Falling weightless once again
Into the chasm,
Bound with chains around her feet.

Stupid fool!
Don't you see?
He's playing a game
You'll never win.
The dancers dance,
Revolving, whirling
Round the deserted ballroom.
Ghosts of the past
Draw them deeper,
Into the clutches
Of the grinning enemy.
A touch,
And hope slinks hopelessly
Into shadows too dark, too deep.
You knew, didn't you?
He would win,
Hands down.

The phone rings.
She responds.

Get Up and Go!

So here we are.
God's been and gone and done it.
Success on a plate,
Light at the end of a long dark tunnel.

But hang on a mo'…
Where's that radiant smile?
What's with the frown?
Have you messed up somewhere?

You see, you're healed.
Free to go.
Free to serve.
So light up and live
For God's sake.
What's up woman?
Don't you understand?
God's got it all in hand.
You're free to go,
The struggling is over.

· ·

But hang on for a minute,
Can I put something to you?
That is, my point of view.
I've lost a limb.

Been wrenched apart,
So have a heart
And give me time.
Just a little more.
I will get there.
Honestly.....?

For You

I had to move a mountain
For you to see your molehill,
And I was left in pieces,
For you to be made whole.
I had to make a journey,
And be battered, soiled and wearied.
You just followed in my footsteps
To find peace for your soul.

My path was full of boulders,
And I had to fight resistance.
I had to carry guilt and pain,
Responsibility.
I pushed and heaved in earnest,
Tried so hard to get it right,
Fingers ached from picking locks,
Then I handed you the key.

So, is it good to feel so free of guilt?
Is it good to laugh with joy?
To see rainbows where there once were clouds,
And have serenity?
How I'd love to feel like you do now,
How I should, if life were fair,
But you made me struggle for many a year.
Will I ever be that free?

I'm finding it harder than you to let go,
Now the freedom I strived for is here.
It's so stupid, I feel you laughing out loud,
While I cry still, in anguish and pain.
So be free, and enjoy it, for deep down inside,
I am really pleased for you, my friend.
I am sure I will get there, with God's help and
strength.
It will be worth it, in the end.

Healing?

The peace is here
But sorrow lingers on.
Can peace and sorrow be such close companions?
A paradox?
No. Evidence of healing.

But the grief remains
Like leaden chains
Shudder under their own laborious weight,
Burdened down,
And burdening.

The chains now lifted
Leave a psychosomatic imprint,
So I am still
Unable to move freely-
At present.

Hope commands
That I glance a little further,
Beyond the here and now.
The promise of healing
Stretching vast,
As vast as the horizon.

So to rest,
Allow the weight to lift.
As a hand caught
Under the dead weight of the slumbering
Gradually turns
From stone,
To flesh.
Life returning hurts.
For a short while.

The Secret Life

The secret life
Seems more significant,
More accommodating
To the adulterous mind,
As reason seeps
Slowly
Through the recess of loneliness,
To shelter in the past innocence
Of knowing.
Yet still there appears
Love as lust.
Inconspicuous to all
But the beholder,
And needer.
Vastly occupying,
Deeply missing, all pervading want.
And so to thoughts
And feelings too deep to tell.
Is this a life?

The Lonely Heart

Please don't say I didn't warn you.
Were the signs so obscure?
Threats, but promises,
Fall on deaf ears.
Obliteration
Of the soul's desire.

Please hear the cry
Of a lonely heart.
An uncoping spirit.
Possessed by grief,
Yet turned inward
To the need of the tormentor.
And so onward
To infinity
As a backward glance pleads.

Were it not
For the infiltration of life,
The pounding heart
Would alter its lonely rhythm,
And cease.
But yet, still yet,
Pure spirit flows,
And the Trinity invades
The reasoning mind
Heavenward.

To halt the inevitable.
God controls.

The Exposed Heart

The exposed heart
Is a fragile objet d'art,
Vulnerable to the corrosive
Weathering of life.
Buffeted by the winds of change,
And the storms of emotion.
It may be in danger
Of extinction.
Who will care for
This rare creature?
It will take great wealth,
No expense spared,
And drain every last nickel
From the coffers.
But to love
Is to live.
In living we grieve,
Until death.
Let it not be said,
'She did not live'.

Please?

I can't seem to do it,
I can't let go,
Yet I have to say I have.

I have to say I'm fine,
Yet all the time
I'm breaking up inside.

I have to say it's finished.
God's in charge,
Yet it feels so hard to maintain.

I have to say it's OK,
Getting easier by the day.
You can't let God,
Or folk down.

I have to say I'll cope,
But it's so hard to hope
For this dreadful pain to ease.

When the crying never ends,
And loneliness descends,
It gets difficult to maintain the image.

So I have to say I've stopped,
It's getting easier all the time,
But it's really not the truth.

I'm still crying,
Crying,
Crying.
But God knows
I'm really trying.
Won't someone help?
Please?

She Sits Alone

She sits alone
While thoughts pervade
And interrupt the imaginative mind,
Drawing it to a distressing close.
And if she were to speak of thoughts so bleak
Of dread-filled days
That make no sense.
Of curling up in corners,
Foetal-like;
Beyond reach of help or hope.
Riddle talk and nonsense
Mere paraphrase of the bound volume
Contained within,
Unable to be interpreted by an intellectual mind;
Yet not mystical,
Just sad.

Her soul riots,
Tormented by insanity,
Yet outwardly
Normality,
To all but those who know
She sits alone.

Clawing back to reality,
Clinging tightly to the rocky crags of indifference,
While thoughts remain,
And through the pain,
The panic spreads.
Yet hope reaches out, retreats,
Like tendrils, touching, pulling back
As blackness stretches
Endlessly, un-abridged,
Shallow, yet fathomlessly deep.

And if, eventually, she lost all hope,
They'd query why
She had to die.
They didn't know she sat alone
Among the crowds,
And crowded.

To a World in Which Failure is Unacceptable

Posthumously printed,
An epitaph to one
Who reached out in the darkness,
Grasped,
And slipped.

Unrequited pain,
Desperately seeking to adhere
To moral codes.
Yet far-reaching expectations
Never attained.
She tried and failed,
In a world in which failure is unacceptable.

Act 1 Scene 1

The stage is set.
The prisoner
Waits
To be released.

But freedom
Fails to
Make her spectacular entrance.

(Curtain falls)

Listen to the Love of a Family

Grief is a form of love
that is not separated by death

For My Mother R.I.P.

I thought of you last night
As I rode bareback
Through the hazy world of dreams in shades of blue
and black.

And held your head once more
And kissed your lips,
But fingers, slippery eels
Fumbled and let go.
You fell once more, against billowy sheets of white.

And like a child
I needed to clutch at you,
A rag doll,
Tattered and broken in death.

No more to hear the softly spoken words
I longed to hear,
Or feel your gentle breath
Of love
Upon my saddened soul.

To know I am your child,
And you, my mother.

Monsters in the Garden

Can I go outside now?
The child wanted to know,
There are daisies in the garden
And I want to watch them grow.

But there are monsters in the garden,
And they'll eat you up for tea.
You're best to stay inside for now.
Why don't you play with me?

Can I go outside now?
My friends are calling me,
We'll play a game of 'let's pretend'.
They're here now, can't you see?

But there are monsters in the garden,
And they mean to cause you harm.
Tell your friends to come inside,
Where it's safe and warm.

Can I go outside now?
I'm grown up and big,
There are plants and rocks and trees to climb,
And mud for me to dig.

But there are monsters in the garden,
I can't let you out of my sight.
It might be bright and sunny now,
But it will soon be night.

Can I go outside now?
I'm not your baby anymore.
And if you say that I can't go,
I'll just walk out the door.

Have the monsters gone, d'you think?
How will I ever know?
I guess the only way is that.......I'll have to let you go.

Did I Remember to Tell you?

Did I remember to tell you to tidy your room?
To pick up your toys and not leave a mess wherever you go.
Did I remember to tell you to keep down the noise?
When your father's asleep after working all night.

Did I remember to tell you that you can't have a dog?
But you can have a hamster, a rabbit, a cat,
But you didn't want to stop just at that.
So the snakes and the cockatiels, terrapins and frogs
Came along, but remember I told you,
it must stop at dogs.

Did I remember to hug you so tight
when you cried in the night?
From your nightmares and dreams,
And did I remember to tell you so softly
That come the morning, it's not as bad as it seems.

Do you remember that holiday surprise?
When we went to the beach and I told you
Don't get sand in your eyes, but you did,
And it hurt, but the ice-cream made up for the pain,
And we all went again the following year.

Did I remember to tell you to help in the kitchen?
To take out your plate,
and please stop your bitching with siblings,
For it gets on my nerves, and you surely must learn
To get on with each other, as sister and brother.

Did I remember to tell you to be careful of strangers?
There are so many dangers in this world today.
And please do remember this golden rule,
Come straight home from school, as I worry so.

Did I remember to cry when both my girls married?
And when the child you miscarried was so cruelly lost?
That I must have wept over, for it broke your sweet heart,
But I can't remember, was it June or September?
For my memory, you see, has been taken from me.
I am robbed of such beautiful and bittersweet things,
But here is one fact I can never forget,
And neither must you,
I love you
I love you
I passionately do.

Daniel

Sleep, sweet cherub, sleep,
As adoring eyes watch over you.
Your perfect form astounds me,
As human understanding cannot fathom
Such wonderful craftsmanship.

And as you sleep,
Know we love you
For who you are,
For who you may become;
In time, a man, a father, a friend,
Nurtured by your family,
Loved by your sister, Amelie,
And all of us,
Sweet Daniel.

So sleep,
Knowing joy awaits you
When you wake.
And your smile, your laugh,
Thrills us- such joyousness
In one so young!
My perfect one,
Dream on.

William

William, how can I explain
How much joy you bring us?
Your eyes, deep pools,
Fathomless blue, and gentle, too.
A smile that takes my breath away,
Your hair, as fair as new mown hay.
One of God's own angels,
Cherubic, and tender,
Born as the year
Entered its infancy;
You beckoned us all
To join you, in joy,
First of January 2007,
My beautiful boy!
And as you grow,
Know this- we love you,
Cherish you, thank God so much
For your presence here with us,
Making our family complete,
Perfect little William,
My grandson,
My sweet.

For Sweet Amelie

Child of my child,
Formed in the womb
Of a woman- my little girl,
Once within me
But grown now.
I have watched
As her swollen form
Became you, my darling Amelie.

And I have a sense
Of a Russian doll,
The child within the child.
And who may come from you
In many years time?
But another angel to love,
Eternity through maternity,
And I love you all so desperately.

I long to be around for
Each new generation,
But if not, I know
My love, deep and passionate,
Will continue through you,
Child of my child.

Hush Little Child

Hush little child, there's nothing to fear,
Safe from the storm and the wild raging sea.
Far from the monster that lurks in the dark,
Curled in a corner,
My child and I.

Safe from all harm, I'll protect you my dear,
With me as your guardian
There's nothing to fear.
Enfolded by love and surrounded by care,
Curled in a corner,
My child and I.

When the storm passes, we'll venture outside,
Into the sunshine,
We'll test the spring air.
I'll watch as you grow, staying close by your side,
We'll run, laugh and play,
My child and I.

We're far from the coast now,
And up in the hills,
With love all around us,
Safe from all ills.
The past is forgotten, the future ahead,
We'll both grow and develop
Now the monster is dead.

My Child, The Man

My child, the man, is growing,
Cells dividing, multiplying.
Increasing in strength,
Gaining in wisdom,
Pushing firmly against the barriers of childhood,
Into the deep fathomless ocean of adult life.

And I am left,
Bereft.
Hugging a giant; yes, still hugging,
And thanking God we are still hugging.
But fearful of this changeling here in front of me.
Like a vine, a mile a minute,
Future plans,
Careers and colleges,
Girlfriends; a wife and children.
Grandchildren!

But wait!
My child, the man is calling,
Needing strength,
Seeking wisdom.
Loving me- his mother.
So for now, I rest; we pause,
To enjoy a quality of friendship
So precious, so rare.
A forty year old woman, a sixteen year old lad.
In love.
For now – this will do.

Listen to the Pain of Cancer

Cancer came knocking at our front door, we told him to go away, we've been there before.

Together

Last night I watched you sleeping
as I lay restless in my bed.
I thought of all your care
and tenderness over years of being together,
Through joy and pain, laughter and tears.
Now we have a new monster to slay.
Will we manage?
Together.

The very breast that gave life and sustenance
To the children we have borne,
Has turned into a poisonous labyrinth;
Cells charging rampantly through
The gentle ducts of life-giving fluid.
Will we manage?
Together.

We do not know what we will face,
As days turn into agonising weeks,
We will probably cry, laugh
and pray our way through
Difficult decisions, future hopes and dreams
Lay crumpled at our feet.
Will we manage?
Together.

As a strong rope woven out of many strands,
We as a family will survive,
Building new foundations on top of the rubble
That is cancer.
We'll name it and shame it into submission.
Because with our love, we'll manage.
Together, forever.

New Life for Old

And were it not for the beauty of new life,
Would I wither and die
From this canker within?
But no!
Hope strides purposefully,
Head held high,
And holds my hand
Tightly.
Not letting me fail,
But to re-emerge
Stronger than before.
The new knowledge of suffering
Another arrow in the quiver of experience.
Offering new opportunities
That far exceed the expectation.
To be able to come alongside,
Not just caring,
But knowing.
Life uncertain, no longer immortal,
But seen in the context
Of the burgeoning beauty
Of creation.
A babe, a child,
The circle is unbroken.
New life for old.

A Cancer Captive

I stagger from chemotherapy,
Head shaven, a prisoner
Of the captor, cancer.
A tumour multiplying,
Spreading its seed
Beyond my breast, its nest,
A cuckoo spawning death,
And flowing beyond.
Its cargo traversed on rivers
Of blood and lymph,
To distant parts,
But the prison halts its rapid spread,
Yet affects the host,
With a plague that strikes
With sickness, pain and suffering,
Is all of this worth bothering?
But life is worth enduring,
So we fight the battle,

Knowing whatever the outcome,
My time is in God's hands;
He understands my weakness,
And pours out His oil of healing,
On a body scarred and broken,
On fears and doubts unspoken.
So I dare to trust,
And rest in God's presence.

A New Season's Hope

Three seasons now have passed,
And autumn beckons.
So with hope we carefully tread
Among the fallen leaves;
Glorious hues of orange and red.
To leave behind
The cancerous memories;
Hopefully carved out
By the surgeon's hand.
Its remains to die
As summer fades;
Destroyed by poison,
Burned by rays so strong,
To leave a faltering hope
That life will continue along
Its chosen path.
God willing.

Sorry

What does remission mean?
A pause between
Cancer and…..
Cancer?
Waiting for the alien within
To come out from his hiding place.
He managed to avoid
Discovery,
From chemo and radiotherapy,
By hiding in my left toe,
I think.

Then,
As soon as treatment ended,
He reappeared.
Multiplying soundlessly,
Nothing more to fear.
For him.

But me?
More anxiety,
Expectation of recovery
Low.
Zero, in fact,
Not much tact in that,
Is there?

Sorry for the pain
I am causing you all again.
It's hard being loved
By such beautiful people.
I wish with all my soul
That I could exterminate
The alien within,
And return myself
Whole,
To you.

Listen to My Faith

Faith, hope and love;
when faith and hope are lost,
Love remains

On Giving and Receiving

Lord, someone stooped to wash my feet today,
I watched her, mouth wide open, horror-struck,
How could she contemplate this awful task,
For one deemed so unworthy of such love?

She acted in obedience to your word,
And I, like Peter, vowed it could not be,
My feet were sore and blistered, filth ingrained,
For often down the wrong path I had strayed.

In love she gave, so freely, cheerfully giv'n,
Yet I responded wrongly, with a frown,
I felt such deep unworthiness, unclean,
Feet covered with the grime of sin and shame.

Why couldn't I, with gracious, thankful heart
Accept this gift so beautifully bestowed.
With smiles and hugs, and 'Thank you, thank you Lord!'
'Such overwhelming kindness thrills my soul!'

Father, teach me in humility to receive,
As well as to hilariously give,
For as we serve and meet each others needs
We're fulfilling Christ's desire, till he comes.

My precious friend, though 'Thank you' is all I say,
This gift I treasure, stored within my heart,
Unparalleled giving, Christ died for me.
One day my chains will loosen,
I'll be free,
And stand alongside you
In victory!

The Only True Way

Lord, I met with you this morning,
Within the trappings of traditional worship,
Here in the convent.
This surprised me.
Thank you that you transcend all barriers,
All stereotypes, all human pomp and ceremony.
Thank you that you reign supreme,
In this beautiful silent setting.
Yet also in the noisy, modern worship in a school hall.
You reign supreme in the hospital chapel;
And the mud huts of Africa.

Help us to look beyond our human choice,
And know that it is just that....
Human.
Roman Catholic, Pentecostal, Baptist, Evangelical,
Protestant, Quaker.
As long as You are Lord,
The dressing doesn't matter.

Teach us humility.
To appreciate that our way is not the best,
Just different.
Help us to learn from one another,
To respect one another,
To reach out to one another
In Your love.

Because that is the only true way.

Hope is a Flower

A daffodil given
To unsighted eyes
Brings joy
To the beholder,
As colour surrounds,
Encapsulates
The spirit of sunshine.

Hope is a flower,
The colour of joy,
Grown on a crown of thorns.
Painful to grasp,
Scented with the fragrance
Of healing.

The Sower

Lord, I see the sower
Planting seed.
Can't he see what a worthless task he's undertaking?
The strip of ground is so narrow.
Half the fruits of his labour
Fall on concrete.
What's the point?
Lord, I still see him,
Sun's up now.
He toils relentlessly,
To and fro,
To and fro,
No help from anyone
Except the odd crow,
Snatching the seed and carrying it away.
Typical,
He cannot even see the fruits of his labour.
God, how pointless!
Impenitent heat saps his energy,
The rhythm of his swaying hand
Mesmerizes,
To and fro,
To and fro.
He's almost finished,

Task completed.
Poor labourer, what price your constant toiling,
For so little reward?
God knows!

But, on returning, mere months later,
I stand and observe
The outcome.
Lush green fields,
The images in my mind.
At the edge of the field,
Thinly sown,
Weeds have choked it,
Nothing grown.
Waste of time
Yet, wait a while!
Harvest, thickly sown
Is waiting,
Prepared and ready,
Succoured by rich soil,
And sun and rain.
A waste of toil?
NO.
Returned in plenty.
The young sower stands, serene.

Rest Awhile

Silence enters.
An eternity away from roaring traffic,
Chattering children,
Busy shoppers,
The shrill ring of the mobile phone.
No background banter from a ceaseless radio,
Or TV white-noise.
Just stillness.
And into that stillness
Comes the still, small voice,
Of one who loves me.
Calling me, ever so gently,
Calling me,
'You are my beloved.
Rest awhile.'

About the Author

Annie Watkinson has spent much of her life caring for others, most importantly as a wife and mother, but also through nursing, pastoral work in the church and in voluntary work. She now works as a freelance writer, and has written for many nursing journals including *Mental Health Nursing*, *Nursing Times* and *Nursing Standard*, and also for the Christian Magazine, *Woman Alive*. She also spent time on the Editorial Board of *Mental Health Nursing*.

Although Annie has spent many years writing poetry, it was not until her own recent experience of cancer that she decided to publish some of her work. As Annie remarked, "publishing your poetry for others to read is an entirely different experience to publishing articles for specific markets. You are giving away much more of yourself, which can leave you feeling vulnerable and open to criticism."

Annie is currently working on her next book, an autobiography, charting her experiences of living with mental illness and cancer.

Printed in the United Kingdom
by Lightning Source UK Ltd.
127208UK00001B/211-489/P